DID YOU KNOW?

DiNoSAURS LiVE ON!

and other fun facts

For my nephew, John Daniel
—L. D.

To Jackie – Did you finish your homework?
—A. S.

LITTLE SIMON
An imprint of Simon & Schuster Children's Publishing Division
1230 Avenue of the Americas, New York, New York 10020
This Little Simon edition April 2015
Series concept by Laura Lyn DiSiena
For information about special discounts for bulk purchases, please contact Simon & Schuster Special Sales at 1-866-506-1949 or business@simonandschuster.com.
The Simon & Schuster Speakers Bureau can bring authors to your live event. For more information or to book an event, contact the Simon & Schuster Speakers Bureau at 1-866-248-3049 or visit our website at www.simonspeakers.com.
Designed by Ciara Gay
Manufactured in China 0215 SCP
10 9 8 7 6 5 4 3 2 1
Library of Congress Cataloging-in-Publication Data
DiSiena, Laura Lyn, author.
Dinosaurs live on! and other fun facts / by Laura Lyn DiSiena and Hannah Eliot ; illustrated by Aaron Spurgeon. — First edition. pages cm. — (Did you know?) Includes bibliographical references and index.
Audience: 4-8. Audience: K to grade 3.
ISBN 978-1-4814-2425-7 (hc) — ISBN 978-1-4814-2424-0 (pbk) — ISBN 978-1-4814-2426-4 (ebook) 1. Dinosaurs—Juvenile literature. 2. Animals, Fossil—Juvenile literature. 3. Paleontology—Mesozoic—Juvenile literature. I. Eliot, Hannah, author. II. Spurgeon, Aaron, illustrator. III. Title. QE861.5.D569 2015 567.9—dc23 2014013606

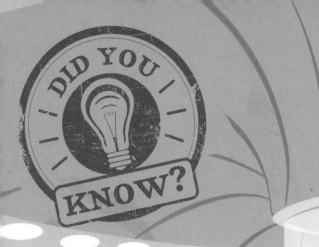

DID YOU KNOW?

DiNOSAURS LiVE ON!

and other fun facts

By Laura Lyn DiSiena and Hannah Eliot
Illustrated by Aaron Spurgeon

LITTLE SIMON
New York   London   Toronto   Sydney   New Delhi

ROAR! Watch out for that TYRANNOSAURUS REX, the dinosaur that was up to 40 feet long and weighed up to 18,000 pounds! Did you know that "Tyrannosaurus" means "tyrant lizard" and that "rex" means "king?"

Did you know that dinosaurs could swim and climb trees? Or that many dinosaurs had natural ways to protect themselves from one another? The Stegosaurus had spikes on its tail, and the Triceratops had three horns on top of its head! Okay, okay. So you knew all those cool facts. But did you know that DINOSAURS LIVE ON?

You may have heard that dinosaurs became extinct around 65 million years ago. Scientists are still trying to figure out what caused this extinction. Some believe that an asteroid collided with Earth. But here's something you might not know. Dinosaurs actually live on in the form of . . . BiRDS! That's right. Scientists have found proof that birds are descendants of a group of dinosaurs called "theropods." Some of the characteristics that link theropod dinosaurs to birds are: hollow bones, sitting on eggs to hatch them, and feathers. So next time you see a bird flying in the air, you can think of it as a living dinosaur!

Have you heard of PTERODACTYLS? You probably know them as the flying dinosaurs, right? Well, the tricky thing is . . . pterodactyls weren't dinosaurs! Pterodactyls were part of a group of flying *reptiles* called "pterosaurs" that were alive at the same time as the dinosaurs. And even though birds are descendants of dinosaurs, prehistoric dinosaurs couldn't actually fly!

JURASSIC

TRIASSIC

Do you know what "prehistoric" means? Prehistoric refers to the time before history started being recorded—the time before writing was even invented. That's a long, LONG time ago. Let's talk about *when* in prehistoric times dinosaurs roamed the earth. Dinosaurs lived during the MESOZOIC era, which began about 250 million years ago and ended 65 million years ago. This era is divided up into the TRIASSIC, JURASSIC, and CRETACEOUS periods.

CRETACEOUS

Scientists have discovered many fossils of the dinosaurs that lived in the Triassic, Jurassic, and Cretaceous periods. Do you know what a fossil is? When an impression or the remains of prehistoric plants and animals are preserved in the earth's crust, the remnant is called a fossil. From fossils, scientists can learn about the skeletons of animals, where the animals lived, how fast they were, and what their skin or hair or feathers were like!

Are you curious about how fossils formed?

Well, for the most part the process went like this: some dinosaurs and other animals got buried by mud or sand right after they died. Over time, sediment covered their remains and encased the parts of the animals that hadn't already rotted away—usually parts such as bones and teeth.

After another long period of time, the chemicals in these buried animals started to change. As the bones and teeth decayed, water that contained minerals seeped into the bones and teeth and replaced the chemicals in them.

This process resulted in a rocklike mineral *copy* of the original bones and teeth.

So what does the word "dinosaur" mean anyway? Well, "dino" means "terrifying" and "sauros" means "lizard." We know that dinosaurs weren't actually *lizards*, but many of them were certainly large and frightening enough to be terrifying!

SAUROPOSEIDON grew to be 60 feet tall, making it the tallest dinosaur.

The BRACHIOSAURUS was one of the heaviest dinosaurs, weighing more than 80 tons. That's the weight of about 17 average-size elephants!

Some of the longest dinosaurs were sauropods. The SEISMOSAURUS, for example, had a long neck and a whip tail. It measured about 110 feet. That's as long as about 3 school buses!

The heaviest single dinosaur bone ever found was one of the backbones of the ARGENTINOSAURUS. The backbone was 5 feet by 5 feet and weighed more than 2,000 pounds.

Are you wondering where on earth all these amazing dinosaurs lived?
Well, there is evidence that dinosaurs lived EVERYWHERE! Maybe even where YOU live!
At the beginning of the age of the dinosaurs, the seven continents were actually arranged together in one SUPERcontinent called Pangaea. Very slowly over time, this supercontinent broke apart into 7 continents and spread across the globe.
And did you know that Earth is still changing? Volcanoes, earthquakes, mountain formation, and sea-floor spreading are all evidence of this.

So dinosaurs even lived in the North and South Poles! BRRR! But this doesn't mean that they needed hats and scarves. When dinosaurs walked the earth, the world was much warmer. Turn the page to find out some of the other places dinosaurs lived!

The first dinosaur bone ever recorded in scientific literature was from a limestone quarry in England.

Many dinosaur fossils have been found in deserts and other remote areas, such as in the Gobi desert in Mongolia, and in the western United States in Arizona, Montana, and Nevada.

Dinosaur fossils dating back to the Triassic period have been found in Brazil.

Recently the world's largest deposit of dinosaur bones— around 7,600 samples—was found in China! That is A LOT of bones!

All of these fossils and bones tell us that some really cool dinosaurs once lived.

Can you believe there was the ANKYLOSAURUS, whose back and sides were covered with steel-like plates? It also had horns behind its eyes and bone plates attached to its skull and jaws. It was basically covered in armor!

There was also the PARASAUROLOPHUS. This dinosaur had a crest on top of its head that contained its hollow tubelike nose cavity. Using this, it created a sound deeper than that of a foghorn!

The OVIRAPTOR was a relative of T. rex and had fancy feathers on its body.

Then there was the KAATEDOCUS, which looked like it was smiling because of the way its teeth were positioned!

And the TRICERATOPS was one of the most dangerous animals to have ever lived. It used the long horns at the top of its head both to attack other dinosaurs and to defend itself.

All right, it's time we talk more about the Tyrannosaurus rex. The T. rex was one of the largest carnivorous dinosaurs that ever lived. In fact, scientists believe that a T. rex could eat as much as 500 pounds of meat in one bite. That's about 2,000 hamburgers!

The T. rex had approximately 50 razor-sharp teeth, small short arms, and scaly skin.

Did you know that the largest tooth of any carnivorous dinosaur found is that of a T. rex?
It would be about 1 foot long if it included the root! This dinosaur had extremely good hearing, vision, and sense of smell—so its prey had to be careful!

The Tyrannosaurus rex lived during the Cretaceous period. Now, here's something that may surprise you. Did you know that there were animals that lived BEFORE the dinosaurs? It's true! Almost 600 million years ago, all creatures lived in the sea. One of the very first predators to exist was the Anomalocaris, which looked like a shrimp covered in armor. After that there was Cameroceras, a huge squid-like animal that lived inside a long, straight shell and grew to be up to 20 feet long. Some scientists who discovered fossils of these shells thought they were fossils of unicorn horns!

Next, animals moved from sea to land. On land there were huge amphibians and giant insects! Meganeura was a large dragonfly-like insect with a wingspan of almost 2 ½ feet!

Around 340 million years ago, the first reptiles evolved. Do you know what a reptile is? Most reptiles are cold-blooded vertebrates, which means they have a backbone or spine. They are usually covered in scales or have a bony external plate, such as a shell. They also typically lay eggs on land. Speaking of shells, can you name a reptile with a shell?

YES! A TURTLE HAS A SHELL!

And can you name a scaly reptile? Here's a hint: it s-s-s-starts with an s-s-s-s . . .

YOU ARE CORRECT! A SNAKE!

Crocodiles, alligators, tortoises, and lizards are all reptiles as well.

Archosaurs were prehistoric reptiles that appeared in the Middle Triassic period. One of the most well-known archosaurs is the ARIZONASAURUS, which lived in Arizona. These reptiles eventually evolved into dinosaurs.

Just as some reptiles evolved into dinosaurs, dinosaurs themselves evolved as well. Even though many dinosaurs were huge, most had pretty tiny brains. Given their size, it's a fact that dinosaurs were some of the dumbest creatures ever to roam this planet. But as time went on, some actually became smarter! The DEINONYCHUS was a dinosaur that hunted in a pack, so scientists believe it knew how to strategize.

CONGRATULATIONS, GRADUATES!

The TROODON was a small dinosaur but is thought to be one of the smartest because its brain was really big for the size of its body. It may have been as intelligent as modern birds. The Troodon is part of the same evolutionary group as the birds of today.

The Troodon was most likely a carnivore, which means it ate meat. But there were plenty of plant-eating dinosaurs—called herbivores—as well . . . and plenty of plants for them to eat. Conifers are the evergreen trees and shrubs that dominated the landscape in the Mesozoic era. There were redwoods, pines, cypress trees, the monkey puzzle tree, and more. Scientists think that flowering plants didn't pop up until the late Jurassic period. Their appearance is linked to a huge boom in the amount of dinosaurs as well! These flowering plants were very nutritious, and allowed plant-eating dinosaurs to grow and reproduce.

Have you ever seen a ginkgo tree? Its leaves are fan-shaped. If you see one of these trees, you're in the presence of a plant that looks almost completely identical to its Mesozoic ancestor!

And it's not only modern *plants* that resemble their ancestors from the age of the dinosaurs. Some species of *animals* alive today actually lived during that age! Certain sea animals, such as the coelacanth fish, are considered "living fossils" because they look so similar to the way they did 360 million years ago. The horseshoe crab, snail, and starfish were *all* living at that time. Crocodiles also evolved and existed alongside the dinosaurs, as did frogs and salamanders. On land, our grasshopper friends were alive way back then. Flies, bees, ants, and butterflies were all witnesses to early dinosaur evolution as well.

So, you see, just as dinosaurs live on in birds, all of these animals that were alive *with* the dinosaurs also LIVE ON!

MORE FUN FACTS

Theropod: The T. rex was actually a theropod!

Pterodactyl: A pterodactyl's wingspan was up to 35 feet!

Dinosaur: Dinosaurs roamed the earth for about 165 million years. In comparison, modern humans (Homo sapiens) have been around for only about 100,000 years!

Reptile: Reptiles use different methods to defend themselves, such as camouflage, hissing, and biting!

South America: Paleontologists believe that some of the very first dinosaurs originated in South America—including the *Saturnalia*, one of the first plant-eating dinosaurs.

Fossil: One type of fossilization occurs when plants or insects are embedded in amber, which is a hardened form of tree resin.

Jurassic period: During the Jurassic period the oceans were filled with sharks, rays, and giant crocodiles.

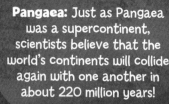

Anomalocaris: When the Anomalocaris died and disintegrated, it tended to separate into different parts. Scientists thought these pieces were individual animals, before realizing they were *parts* of a larger animal!

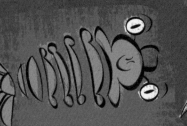

Deinonychus: The Deinonychus was discovered by John Ostrom, the same man who informed the modern theory that birds are descendants of dinosaurs!

Pangaea: Just as Pangaea was a supercontinent, scientists believe that the world's continents will collide again with one another in about 220 million years!

Ankylosaurus: The Ankylosaurus was one of the last dinosaurs to go extinct.

Tyrannosaurus rex: The T. rex had serrated teeth—like a bread knife!

Ginkgo tree: The leaves and nuts produced by ginkgo trees are used for medicinal purposes!

Animals that live on: Many reptile species went extinct a long time ago, but crocodilians have been on the planet for about 200 million years. Today, crocodilians live on in the form of alligators, crocodiles, and more!